Doomsday Scenarios:
Separating Fact from Fiction™

KILLER VIRUSES

Linley Erin Hall

rosen publishing's
rosen central®

New York

Published in 2010 by The Rosen Publishing Group, Inc.
29 East 21st Street, New York, NY 10010

First Edition

Library of Congress Cataloging-in-Publication Data

Hall, Linley Erin.
Killer viruses / Linley Erin Hall.
    p. cm.—(Doomsday scenarios: separating fact from fiction)
Includes bibliographical references and index.
ISBN 978-1-4358-3561-0 (library binding)
ISBN 978-1-4358-8524-0 (pbk)
ISBN 978-1-4358-8525-7 (6 pack)
1. Virus diseases—Juvenile literature. I. Title.
RA644.V55H35 2010
616.9'1—dc22

                                                                              2009018167
Manufactured in Malaysia

CPSIA Compliance Information: Batch #TWW10YA: For Further Information contact Rosen Publishing, New York, New York at 1-800-237-9932

On the cover: A doctor wearing protective clothing checks a patient with swine flu in early 2009. Although the swine flu outbreak was frightening, it did not turn out to be as deadly a disease as the 1918 flu.

CONTENTS

Introduction

It's September. Students are back in school, and the first hint of fall is in the air. Illness is in the air, too. In communities around the world, a lot of people are getting sick. Very sick.

For John, like for most people, it starts with a dull headache. Then his eyes start to burn. Chills come next. He shivers violently, curled up in bed under heavy blankets. John's high fever refuses to break. His muscles ache. He drifts in and out of sleep. Both awake and asleep, he feels he is trapped in a nightmare that won't end.

Slowly, John's face turns a deep purple color and his feet turn black. He begins to cough up blood, the foamy red spittle clinging to his lips. He gasps for breath. Doctors can do nothing but watch while John fights for his life. He soon loses that fight.

Other people have come down with this flu. Some of them die within hours. They are healthy at breakfast but gone by dinnertime. Others die more slowly, over days. Those who survive are incredibly weak. They may keep to their beds for weeks, even months.

During an epidemic of a killer virus, there may be more patients in hospital beds. Other spaces, such as schools and gymnasiums, may be turned into makeshift emergency medical clinics.

In an attempt to halt the spread of the killer disease, cities close schools, theaters, churches, and other places where people gather in large numbers. People wear masks over their mouths and noses when they go out, if they go out at all. Some businesses shut down because their employees are too afraid to go to work. In some communities, it becomes illegal to cough or shake hands in public. Other cities close their exit and entrance points, such as bridges and tunnels and major highways. No one is allowed in or out. Many

During a pandemic, many people wear masks that cover their mouth and nose when in public. This may help reduce transmission of the disease.

countries censor the media—officials don't want people to know how widespread and deadly the illness is.

Hospitals run out of beds. School gymnasiums and community centers are turned into makeshift medical centers. But there are not enough doctors and nurses to care for all the patients. Some medical personnel also begin to suffer from the disease. Others refuse to go to work for fear of getting sick.

Many morgues are filled to overflowing, with bodies stacked in piles. Funeral homes run out of caskets. People place the dead in simple wooden or cardboard boxes or in cloth sacks. In some places, funerals are prohibited, since any human gathering has the potential to spread the disease.

About half the people in the world become infected. Of those, about 5 percent die. The disease mostly kills children under five, the elderly, and young, healthy adults in their twenties and thirties. Many children lose their parents and are orphaned.

This nightmarish scenario sounds like something out of a science fiction story. But it actually happened. In 1918, an influenza pandemic swept the world. Exact death counts are not known, but an estimated fifty to one hundred million people died in only eight weeks.

The world has learned a lot in the last ninety years. Have we learned enough? How likely is it that an outbreak of such a disease could occur again? And, if it happened, would it really cause such devastation?

Chapter 1

A VIRUS INVADES

People catch minor respiratory illnesses all the time. These colds include coughing, sneezing, and sore throats. Some diseases are much more serious, however.

Most people get sick at least once or twice a year. Usually, the illness is just a cold. After a few days of a runny nose and a cough, most people feel better. Other common infectious diseases include the flu, strep throat, and ear infections. An infectious disease is one that is caused by organisms such as viruses or bacteria. It spreads from person to person or, in some cases, from animals to people. Noninfectious diseases do not spread from person to person. For example, cancer and heart disease are not infectious.

The infectious diseases that are most common in the United States today are usually mild. Improvements in sanitation and medical care have drastically reduced or even eliminated cases of many infectious diseases in the United States. However, new diseases continue to arise, and some of these are deadly.

Some people believe that a large outbreak of an extremely deadly infectious disease is likely to occur soon. An outbreak occurs when multiple people in an area get the same infectious disease at the same time. One person gets sick, he or she passes on the disease to friends, family members, classmates, and coworkers, and soon a lot of people are ill. Outbreaks of infectious disease, which are also called epidemics, happen frequently. Usually, they are small, or the disease is mild. A large or deadly epidemic, however, could be very difficult for the health care system to deal with.

Two different scenarios of a deadly epidemic are possible. In one, a natural virus becomes much more dangerous to humans. This is what happened in the 1918 flu pandemic described in the introduction (a pandemic is a global epidemic). In the second scenario, terrorists deliberately release a virus to frighten and weaken their enemies. Such bioterrorist attacks have occurred, though viruses were not used. For example, in 2001, seventeen people became sick and five died when a terrorist sent letters contaminated with anthrax—a bacterium—to several news media offices and the offices of two U.S. senators.

In order to explain the way that a virus works and how it infects healthy people, making them unwell, this chapter looks at an outbreak of a mild disease in a middle school. It starts with Ryan, who isn't feeling well.

A Sampling of Viral Diseases

Viruses cause many different diseases. Here are a few that are familiar and some that are not so familiar but could be very dangerous if an outbreak occurred:

- **Chicken pox:** This disease involves fever and an itchy rash. A vaccine is available to prevent chicken pox infection.
- **Influenza:** Also known as the flu, influenza comes in many strains. Seasonal flu causes a mild illness. Researchers think that flu viruses currently found in birds could cause a pandemic like the one in 1918.
- **Hantavirus:** Mice transmit this virus to humans. Symptoms include muscle aches, fever, cough, and difficulty breathing.
- **Ebola:** This disease involves fever, headache, red eyes, and abdominal pain, progressing to vomiting, bloody diarrhea, and bleeding from the mouth and nose. Outbreaks have killed 50 to 90 percent of victims.

Here, a scientist collects specimens from trapped rodents to determine if they carry hantavirus. In humans, this virus can be deadly.

- **Human immunodeficiency virus (HIV)/Acquired immune deficiency syndrome (AIDS):** This sexually transmitted infection attacks the immune system, leaving victims more vulnerable to other infections. Drugs slow the disease but cannot cure it.
- **Smallpox:** This disease involves fever, weakness, headache, and a distinctive rash. In the twentieth century, smallpox killed about three hundred million people. Thanks to vaccination, smallpox no longer exists in nature.
- **Measles:** This disease involves fever, loss of appetite, coughing, and a rash. Although measles can cause death, people with this disease are more likely to die from opportunistic infections.
- **Severe acute respiratory syndrome (SARS):** This disease is like a really bad version of the common cold. An outbreak in 2002–2003 killed hundreds of people.
- **Yellow fever:** Transmitted by mosquitoes, this disease includes high fever, headache, nausea, vomiting, and jaundice (the skin turns yellow). The disease used to be common in the southern United States but is now found mainly in Africa and South America.

The Biology of Viruses

Ryan wakes up Tuesday morning with a runny nose, scratchy throat, and a cough. He doesn't have a fever, but his mom decides he should stay home from school. After taking a decongestant, Ryan goes back to bed.

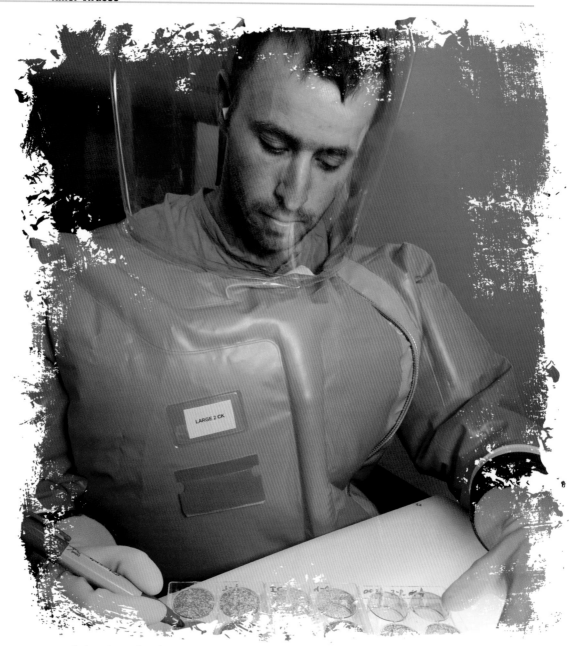

Scientists who do research on highly deadly viruses must wear protective suits and conduct their experiments in specialized laboratories. This helps ensure that they do not become infected.

Inside Ryan's body, a virus is taking over his cells. A virus is a piece of nucleic acid surrounded by a protein shell. There are two types of nucleic acids: DNA and RNA. DNA contains the instructions for creating the proteins that do the work in cells. RNA is created in an intermediate step in the process that, in cells, builds proteins from the instructions contained within DNA.

A virus is not a cell, however. Viruses are parasites that take over cells. They cannot survive on their own. Viruses use cells from organisms to create more viruses. This often causes disease.

When Ryan first became infected, a virus particle entered his nose and attached itself to one of his throat cells. Then it injected its nucleic acid into the cell. Once inside, the virus took over the machinery of the cell. It directed the cell to make new virus particles, instead of the usual proteins. After several hours, the diseased cell burst, releasing the new virus particles so that they could take over more cells.

Fortunately, a virus can't attach to just any cell. Viruses have certain proteins on their surfaces that recognize specific proteins on the surfaces of cells. Thus, a virus may only be able to infect lung cells and not intestinal cells, for example. Or a virus may be able to infect the cells of humans but not those of animals.

The Body Fights Back

As Ryan sleeps, his body works hard to defend itself against the invading virus. The primary defender is the immune system. It pumps out special cells that identify the virus and attempt to kill it. Some of these cells are generic. They can

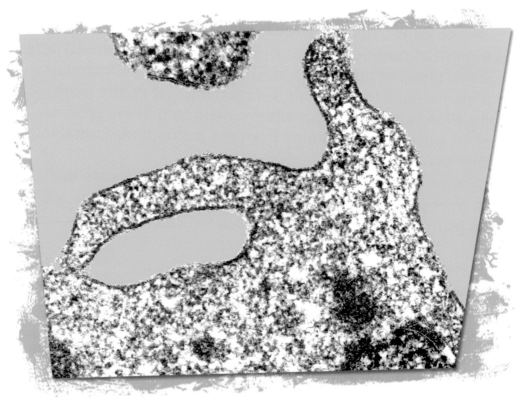

This gray blob is a white blood cell that is attacking invading bacteria (green blobs). By engulfing and destroying the invaders, the white blood cell (part of the immune system) helps prevent disease.

be used against any invader. Other cells are specific to the particular virus that is invading the body. These specific cells have proteins called antibodies on their surfaces. Each antibody recognizes a specific invader.

In addition to killing the virus, the body kills some of its own cells to prevent them from becoming infected or to stop them from making more virus particles. In some cases, however, the body kills too many cells, which can kill the person. This is why so many people in their twenties and thirties died in the 1918 flu pandemic. Their immune systems worked too well. In killing off the virus, their immune systems actually killed them as well.

Bacteria, Antibiotics, and Antivirals

That afternoon, Ryan's mom is worried about his cough, so she takes him to see the doctor. After a short examination, Dr. Moore says that Ryan probably just has a bad cold. She suggests that the boy stay home, rest, and drink lots of fluids. Ryan's mom asks about antibiotics. Dr. Moore reminds her that antibiotics are effective only against bacterial infections and that viruses, not bacteria, cause colds.

Viruses are not the only organisms that cause infectious diseases. Bacteria are single-celled creatures that cause illnesses such as step throat. Bacteria can also make viral infections worse. When a virus invades the body, the immune system tries to get rid of it. If a virus is distracting the immune system, bacteria have an easier time getting around the body's overworked defenses and causing illness. For example, some flu patients also come down with pneumonia, a bacterial infection. Many of the people who died in the 1918 flu pandemic actually died not from the flu but from pneumonia. A disease that takes hold while the immune system is distracted with another invader is called an opportunistic infection.

Doctors treat bacterial infections with medications called antibiotics. These drugs target cell components that bacteria have but animal cells do not. Unfortunately, since viruses don't have these cell components either, antibiotics do not harm viruses.

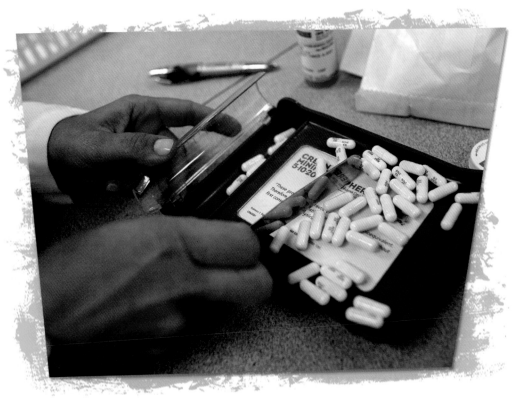

These pills are antibiotics, which are used to treat infections caused by bacteria. Antibiotics are useless against diseases caused by viruses.

Doctors sometimes use other medications, called antivirals, to treat viral infections. But there aren't many antiviral drugs. Viruses are just nucleic acid and protein. All cells also contain nucleic acids and proteins. Thus, it's hard to create a drug that will kill a virus without harming human cells, too. Most antivirals do not actually kill the virus. They simply slow it down, which gives the immune system more time to launch an effective defense.

Most people with viral infections receive only supportive care. This is treatment that does not kill the virus but helps the patient be more comfortable and fight off the disease. An example of supportive care is providing fluids to prevent dehydration in a patient with diarrhea.

Vaccination

As Ryan and his mom are leaving the doctor's office, a nurse reminds them that Ryan is due for his next measles vaccine. She asks them to make an appointment when Ryan is well.

Vaccinations help prevent people from getting certain viral infections. Unfortunately, the protection that vaccines offer does not last a lifetime. Also, vaccinations are not available for many diseases.

One way to protect against viral diseases is through vaccination. During vaccination, a doctor exposes a person to a small amount of a virus. Usually, vaccines are injected, but a few are swallowed. This virus in the vaccine may be already dead, or it may be a very weak strain that cannot cause severe disease. Some newer vaccines contain only parts of viruses. The body reacts to the vaccine by producing antibodies. If the person later comes in contact with the actual virus, the body is prepared to attack it with these antibodies. So the person either will not become sick or will come down with a very mild case of the disease.

However, the immunity provided by vaccines does not last forever. Many vaccines require booster shots after a period of time. Many adults do not get these booster shots, so they are at risk of infection. Also, vaccines are not available for many diseases. The common cold is one of these.

The Virus Spreads

Two days later, Ryan is feeling much better, though he is still coughing. He asks his mom if he can go to school. He's worried about missing too many rehearsals for the school play

This photograph, taken with a special high-speed camera, shows how far droplets of mucus from a sneeze can fly. If other people inhale this aerosol, they can become sick as well.

and doesn't want to fall too far behind in his classes. His mom agrees. In his first-period science class, Ryan finds that Sara, his lab partner, is out sick. His best friend, Oliver, is absent as well. Ryan isn't the only person in the class with a cold either. It seems like not a minute goes by without some-one coughing or sneezing.

Infectious diseases spread from person to person in many ways. Many common diseases, like colds, are transmitted through the air. A sick person coughs or sneezes, releasing tiny droplets of mucus that contain virus particles. This is known as an aerosol. A healthy person breathes the air containing the aerosol and becomes sick. Diseases can also be transmitted if someone gets an aerosol on their hands and then touches their eyes or nose.

Some illnesses are transmitted through contact with bodily fluids, including saliva, blood, semen, and vaginal fluid. Other diseases are passed on through contaminated food or water. Finally, animals, particularly blood-sucking insects such as mosquitoes, can transmit some diseases between people.

It makes sense that the people closest to Ryan are the most likely to catch his cold. They're the ones who are nearby when he sneezes or coughs. In this way, diseases can race through families and communities. But a common cold going around a middle school is not cause for panic. The next chapter looks at some scenarios for much larger outbreaks of more serious diseases.

Chapter 2

DEADLY VIRAL OUTBREAK SCENARIOS

Officials at a hospital in Singapore screen visitors with a thermal scanner. They are trying to prevent anyone who may be ill with SARS from infecting patients whose immune systems are already busy fighting other diseases.

Given what we know about viruses and epidemics, what could happen if a deadly new disease appeared in the world? Optimists suggest that we have the resources to identify and treat a new virus before it becomes a major problem. Pessimists say that we are very unprepared and should expect massive death and destruction.

The rest of this chapter looks at three chilling scenarios concerning disease outbreaks.

A Deadly Cold

People in southern China start turning up in emergency rooms with high fevers, fatigue, and terrible coughs. Some have fluid in their lungs, and some die. They test negative for influenza. The disease stumps physicians. A frightened public buys all available antibiotics, leading to shortages.

The Chinese government keeps the outbreak a secret. Officials fear that if people know that a new disease is on the loose, China will lose business from tourism. When contacted by the World Health Organization (WHO), the Chinese Ministry of Health explains that there is merely a small outbreak of seasonal flu.

One of the physicians treating patients with the strange new disease goes to Hong Kong to attend a wedding. Two days into his trip, it becomes clear that he has contracted the same disease as his patients. The doctor goes to the hospital. He warns the staff that he is probably highly contagious, but they do not take his warning seriously.

People who stayed in the same hotel as the physician return home to many different countries. There, they start to become ill as well, passing on the virus to others. Within a few weeks, people in seventeen different countries have the disease. No one knows exactly how the virus is passed from person to person, but people keep getting sick. The doctors and nurses caring for patients often become ill. This suggests that the disease requires close contact. On the other hand, most of the hotel guests don't remember ever meeting the sick doctor. This suggests that casual contact—a sneeze in a hallway—might be enough to spread the disease.

Researchers work feverishly to identify the virus that causes the disease. They test mucus samples from patients against antibodies from every known disease-causing organism. All the tests turn up nothing. The disease is completely new.

Eventually, scientists identify a coronavirus as the culprit. Usually, coronaviruses cause the common cold, a mild illness. This one, however, somehow turned deadly. After a few months, physicians and public health workers are able to get the disease under control. But during the outbreak, more than eight thousand people became sick. Nearly eight hundred died.

This nightmare scenario actually happened in 2002–2003. The disease is known as severe acute respiratory syndrome, or SARS. The epidemic terrified many people. But SARS did not become a pandemic like the 1918 flu. The next chapter looks at some of the reasons why.

Super Smallpox

The crowd goes wild! Fans from all over the United States—and the world—have come together to cheer on their favorite team in the Super Bowl. But some spectators aren't just cheering. A handful of "fans" have entered the stadium holding small amounts of the smallpox virus in devices that look like the inhalers that people with asthma use when they're having trouble breathing. When the terrorists, pretending to cheer, lift their arms overhead, they also give the devices a pump. This releases the smallpox virus in aerosol form.

Usually, smallpox transmission requires close contact with an infected person or items the person has used. However, the terrorists have engineered a strain that will float in the air for a long time. All around the stadium, fans breathe in the smallpox particles. The next day, they go to the airport and fly back to their homes. Smallpox has an incubation period of twelve to fourteen days. Thus, two weeks after the Super Bowl,

Pittsburgh Steelers fans cheer their team, which is playing against the Arizona Cardinals in Super Bowl XLIII. Places where large crowds gather, such as sporting events, can be tempting targets for bioterrorists.

people begin arriving in emergency rooms and doctors' offices with fevers, headaches, backaches, and rashes.

Naturally occurring smallpox was globally eradicated in the 1970s. Most physicians have never seen or treated a case

of it in their professional lives. Thus, people are first diagnosed with other ailments, such as chicken pox. After several days, an ER doctor in the Super Bowl host city finally recognizes that a smallpox outbreak has occurred. When he tries to report it to public health officials, however, they do not believe him at first.

By this point, thousands more people have been exposed to the virus. Because smallpox no longer exists in nature, most people are not vaccinated for it. Those who were vaccinated years ago, before the disease was eradicated, likely have no immunity to it anymore. The United States has some smallpox vaccine left over from the 1970s, but it's not nearly enough. It's so old that no one knows if it will even work anymore. Furthermore, no antiviral medications are known to be effective against smallpox. Even with supportive care, smallpox kills about a third of its victims. Panic ensues.

Government agencies waste precious time arguing about who should be in charge of the response. Because the small-pox obviously came from a terrorist group, rather than arising naturally, the military seizes control. The first thing it does is institute quarantines—areas of isolation for smallpox patients and the people they may have exposed to the virus. In some cases, this means sealing off entire cities—no one enters or exits. Soldiers shoot people who try to get past their roadblocks.

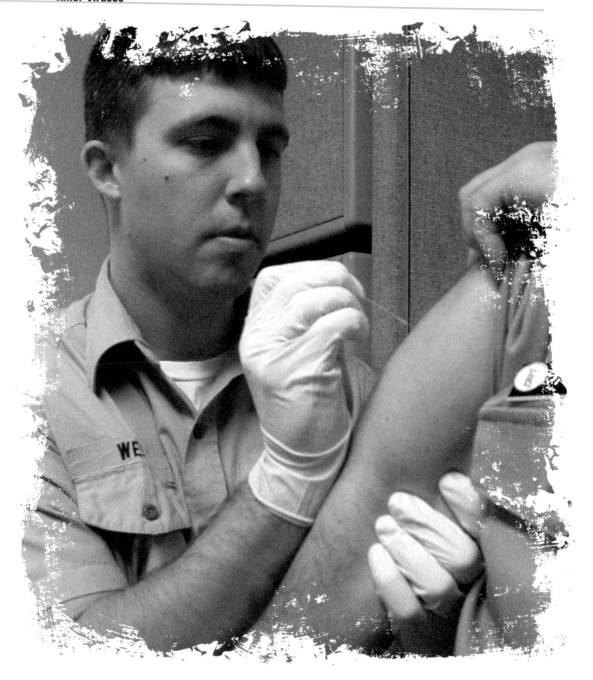

Vaccines for smallpox are given with a special three-pronged needle. Special training is required to be able to administer the vaccine correctly.

Particular hospitals are designated for smallpox victims. The military vaccinates the health care workers who will serve in these hospitals. Some doctors and nurses experience severe side effects from the vaccine. In others, the vaccine doesn't work, and they fall ill. The result is a shortage of medical personnel to care for patients, which increases the number of deaths.

People flee cities not under quarantine, afraid that cases of smallpox will be identified there and exits will be closed. But the military does not have enough soldiers to enforce a quarantine in every city. When it becomes apparent that smallpox is everywhere, borders reopen. No one is safe from the disease. Pharmaceutical companies start to work on new smallpox vaccines, but new drug development typically takes years of research and testing. Smallpox kills its victims quickly, so any new drug will be ready far too late. Meanwhile, the members of the terrorist group responsible for the smallpox attack are watching the drama unfold on television, celebrating their success and the havoc they've created.

Avian Flu

The first to die are a bunch of chickens. The huge shed on the poultry farm contains thirty thousand chickens being raised for the dinner table. The chickens begin coughing. Soon, they are coughing up blood. Eventually, they fall over dead. When workers cut open the dead birds, they find that their internal organs look like Jell-O. The company, worried about bad publicity and lost profits, decides not to report the outbreak. Instead, it processes the still-living birds into meat as fast as possible, before they can either be infected or show signs of the disease.

Avian flu has been a problem in poultry for many years. In some cases, the virus can jump from birds to humans. Here, signs warn people in Hong Kong not to touch live poultry at a market.

But the virus spreads to other sheds on the poultry farm, and then to other farms in the area. Then some of the poultry workers start coughing. They develop fevers, headaches, fatigue, burning eyes, and chills. Since the workers don't

report for their jobs, they don't know that others are also sick. Nor do they think that they may have the same disease as the birds. Those who see a doctor are told that they have the flu. And they do. But it's not seasonal flu.

The workers' family members and friends start to become ill as well. Some people seem to have only a touch of the seasonal flu. Others are gravely ill, struggling to breathe as their lungs fill with fluid. Three die in the same hospital. They are all young men in their twenties who were perfectly healthy just a week before. The attending physician calls the Centers for Disease Control and Prevention (CDC), declaring, "We've got an avian influenza outbreak."

Meanwhile, in ten different states, people have bought chicken from the infected farms. Influenza mostly attacks the lungs of humans. In birds, however, it mainly attacks the intestines. Thus, feces (solid waste) can spread the virus. Chicken meat sometimes has traces of fecal matter on it. If the chicken is improperly cooked or if someone handling raw chicken touches their eyes, nose, or mouth, the virus can spread from the meat to humans. And it does.

Many avian flu outbreaks have occurred in poultry since the late 1990s. Sometimes, the virus infected humans. Those avian flu viruses were not good at moving from one human to another. This virus, however, is very good at it.

Animal Diseases

I had a little bird,
Its name was Enza.
I opened the window,
And in-flu-enza.

In 1918, girls jumped rope while chanting this rhyme. Though they didn't know that the worldwide influenza pandemic currently raging through their neighborhoods was due to a virus that started in a bird, their nursery rhyme was not far off the mark. In general, the new viral diseases that have appeared in humans in recent decades have jumped from animals to people.

An animal that carries a virus that doesn't harm the animal is called a reservoir. For example, ducks are the natural reservoir for the influenza virus. Influenza lives in the duck's intestines without harming it.

Viruses make small changes in their DNA all the time. Some of these changes make it easier for them to infect a new species. For example, a duck has never been known to give a human the flu. But changes in the duck influenza virus that make it better able to infect chickens also make it more able to infect humans. Thus, the chickens are infected by ducks, and these infected chickens, in turn, pass the disease on to people.

The CDC sounds the alarm, but it's too late. The virus has already infected too many people in too many places, and it moves too efficiently. Early victims, not yet realizing they are sick, have traveled on planes and trains. The virus hops from person to person in crowded airports. The recirculating air on airplanes spreads the virus to even more people. Travelers take influenza off the plane with them when they land, infecting friends, family, and coworkers. Within days, reports of illness start cropping up in every major city on the planet.

The sound of coughing can be heard everywhere, constantly. As patients' lungs fill with fluid, they need respirators to stay alive. But soon all respirators are in use. Every ICU (intensive care unit) bed is full. To make matters worse, some health care workers stop showing up for work, afraid of becoming sick themselves. Hospitals turn patients away. Many people don't even bother to try to get medical care. The disease kills anywhere from a third to half of its victims.

There is no vaccine for bird flu. Researchers begin working to develop one, but it will not be ready for four to six months. Antiviral drugs, such as Tamiflu, offer some protection. But supplies of Tamiflu are extremely limited. People argue about how and to whom the medication should be distributed. Children first? Health care workers first? Those with lots of money or influence first?

Many people panic. The stock market crashes. People who are still healthy flee the cities where there is bird flu. Those who have vacation homes in rural areas hide there. Many people stop going to work or begin working from home. Some officials suggest killing every chicken in the world to stop the spread of bird flu. But it's far too late for that. The virus has long since made the leap from chickens to humans, and humans are now infecting each other.

Chapter 3

REDUCING THE LIKELIHOOD OF A KILLER EPIDEMIC

A mosquito feeds on the blood of a human. Mosquitoes transmit many diseases, including West Nile virus. This virus has become a problem in the United States in recent years.

The thought of a large outbreak of a deadly disease, such as smallpox or bird flu, is a frightening one. However, many respected scientists and public health officials from the CDC, WHO, and other groups think it could happen. Some are even sure that it will happen. The question for them is not if, but when and how bad will it be?

When the next killer pandemic will occur is unpredictable. But its severity is much more under our control. We are more prepared for a pandemic or bioterrorist attack than we were a few years ago. The anthrax attacks in 2001, the SARS outbreak in 2003, and the many bird flu outbreaks among poultry in the last decade have raised awareness about epidemics. Governments have begun to act. They have stockpiled drugs, funded research for new vaccines, and trained police, public health workers, and others likely to be on the front lines of the war against a new epidemic.

More work needs to be done. We are not as prepared as we could or should be. But there is good news. Because of the efforts so far, and the characteristics of viral reproduction, the worst nightmare scenarios are unlikely to occur.

A Virus's Reproductive Rate

An outbreak of a new disease could be very dangerous. However, it is unlikely to wipe out half the world's population in a month. This is because of the ways that diseases spread.

A disease's reproductive rate is determined by the number of other people that a sick person usually infects. It's a measure of how contagious the disease is. The reproductive rate depends on several variables. One is the severity of the illness. People who are very sick stay in bed. They interact with very few people. Thus, they can infect very few other people. People with milder illnesses often continue to go to work or school. This allows the disease to spread more widely.

A virus's reproductive rate also depends on how it is transmitted from person to person. Diseases that are spread through the air, by coughing or sneezing, tend to have higher reproductive rates. A disease that is spread by contaminated food or water, insects, or blood or other bodily fluids generally has a lower reproductive rate.

How hardy the virus is also plays a role. Some viruses can live only while in a nice, moist glob of mucus. Once the mucus dries, the virus dies. Other viruses are much stronger. For example, a smallpox virus that resides on a dry surface that is out of the sun can survive for weeks or even months.

Scientists think that measles and influenza have reproductive rates around thirty or forty. This means that one person with the flu can infect, on average, forty other people. SARS, on the other hand, has a reproductive rate of less than two. This is one reason why the SARS outbreak was not any worse. The disease wasn't very contagious.

The most serious disease in an epidemic would be one that is very hardy, is spread through the air, is mild long enough for victims to spread it around, but still kills a lot of people. Fortunately, few diseases have all of these characteristics.

Closely Watched Diseases

Chapter 2 describes past outbreaks of two diseases that are top contenders for new killer epidemics: avian influenza and smallpox. Bird flu is the most likely cause of a future naturally occurring pandemic (as opposed to a human-engineered pandemic, released by terrorists, for example). Outbreaks of highly deadly avian influenza have occurred in chickens and other domestic poultry since the late 1990s. Millions of birds have been killed to stop these flu viruses from racing through the world's poultry farms. Although farmers have tried to keep some outbreaks of avian flu a secret, monitoring and reporting of the disease have improved in recent years.

These bird flus have infected some people. However, none of the viruses have been very good at moving from human to human. Human outbreaks have been small as a result. In early 2009, a swine flu epidemic occurred. Birds can infect pigs with influenza. Pigs can then pass it on to humans. The swine flu infected tens of thousands of people, but it was not as deadly as some researchers predict a bird flu epidemic could be. Experts believe that a bird flu virus could someday develop the ability to move between humans more easily and that this could cause a pandemic.

Other possible causes of future naturally occurring pandemics include SARS and hemorrhagic fevers, such as Ebola and Lassa fevers. Hemorrhagic fevers cause people to bleed profusely and are quite gruesome. Larger outbreaks of Ebola (more than a handful of people) have typically killed 50 to 90 percent of those infected. But symptoms of the disease appear soon after infection, and people become very sick very quickly, limiting their ability to unknowingly infect friends, family members, and coworkers. Furthermore, transmission of hemorrhagic fevers requires close and intimate contact. This means that outbreaks of the disease are easier to control and are less likely to cause a pandemic.

SARS was a frightening epidemic because the disease was new and scientists took so long to identify it. Although public health officials brought it under control, the virus could emerge again. However, the SARS virus would need to increase its reproductive rate before it could truly cause a pandemic. Of course, there is the possibility that a completely new virus could arise to start a pandemic. But, in the meantime, bird flu is the one to worry about as a naturally occurring pandemic.

Other diseases are of concern in the context of bioterrorist attacks. The CDC maintains a list of the poisons, bacteria, and

Ebola is one of the most feared diseases because of how deadly it is. Here, a worker disinfects villagers who have attended the funeral of an Ebola victim in the African country of Uganda.

viruses that are most dangerous if used as weapons. The CDC's category A (highest priority) list includes two viral diseases—smallpox and hemorrhagic fevers. As mentioned above, hemorrhagic fevers could also cause a natural epidemic. However, since it has been eradicated in nature since the 1970s, any outbreak of smallpox would definitely be a human-engineered act of biological warfare.

The WHO declared smallpox to be eradicated in 1979. No natural cases have occurred in more than three decades. However, samples of smallpox still exist in laboratories. Physicians were supposed to destroy any smallpox they had or send it either to the CDC in Atlanta or to the Institute for Viral Preparations in Russia. It's possible that some labs did not do this. Smallpox samples might have been stolen from the Russian laboratory as well. Thus, terrorists might be able to obtain smallpox and use it as a weapon. And because no one has been vaccinated for smallpox in thirty years, the human population is extremely vulnerable to infection. The virus could be extremely dangerous and very deadly.

Several different kinds of viral encephalitis could also be used as biological weapons. These mosquito-borne diseases cause acute inflammation (swelling) of the brain, which can result in coma or death. The death rate varies depending on the particular virus, but it can be more than 30 percent. However, since these diseases are transmitted from person to person through mosquitoes, rather than through direct human contact, the CDC considers them less of a threat.

The Likelihood of Bioterrorism

Unfortunately, the knowledge needed to grow a virus for use in a terrorist attack is available to anyone who studies

The Smallpox Vaccine

The U.S. government has enough smallpox vaccine for everyone in the country. And yet, it's not available to the general public. Only health care workers and emergency responders have received it. Why isn't everyone lining up to get the shot? There are three reasons.

First, the vaccine can cause life-threatening complications. Until an outbreak of smallpox is confirmed, receiving the vaccine may be more dangerous than not receiving it. Second, the vaccine offers full protection for only three to five years. It's a lot to ask people to get a shot every five years just in case of a terrorist attack that may never actually occur. Third, the vaccine can prevent smallpox or make it milder if received within three days of exposure to the virus. If a bioterrorist quietly unleashes a smallpox attack, the vaccine won't help those who are the first to unknowingly fall ill because smallpox has such a long incubation period. They will become sick and aware of their condition after the optimal three-day vaccine treatment period. But the vaccine will benefit most of the population once it becomes known that the smallpox virus has been released.

biology. The same techniques and equipment that are used to grow viruses for useful applications, such as vaccines, are also used to grow viruses for weapons. Preparing a virus that will infect a lot of people is very difficult, but it is still possible with enough time and effort.

It is important to keep in mind, however, that terrorists primarily want to spread fear through the general population,

In 2001, letters containing anthrax were sent through the U.S. mail. Although few people died, many were terrified that their mail would be contaminated as well.

disrupt people's daily lives, and destroy their morale. This does not necessarily require a lot of people to die or even become infected. In the 2001 anthrax mail attacks, only twenty-two people became sick, five of whom died. But thousands of people took antibiotics, and millions were terrified to open their mail. The impact and disruption were huge. Thus, if fear and disturbance are the goals, a small outbreak can be as effective as a larger one. Furthermore, as the attacks on September 11, 2001, demonstrated, terrorists can cause widespread fear using more ordinary, "everyday" objects (such as hijacked commercial airplanes and box cutters) as weapons, which require far less time, money, and expertise to prepare than biological weapons do.

Government Response to Epidemics

In recent years, the U.S. government has increased its efforts to prepare for a bioterrorist attack or naturally occurring epidemic. Emergency response plans specific to avian influenza and smallpox are available online. Many health care workers, military personnel, and emergency responders, such as police and firefighters, have received training in how to respond to an outbreak. They have also learned what

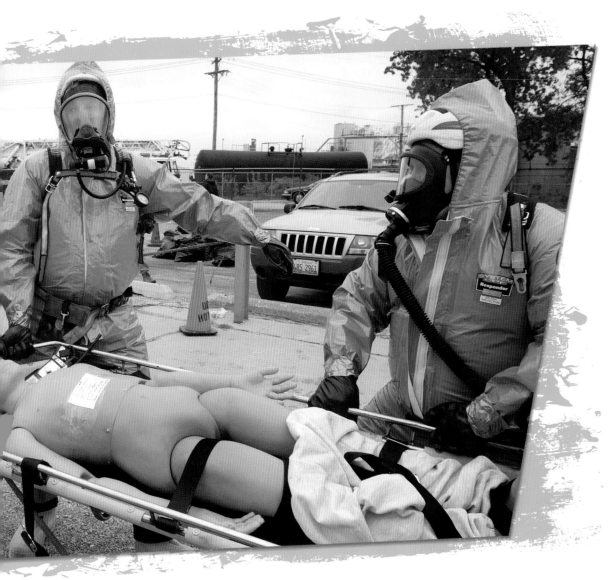

In this training exercise, rescue workers move victims to a decontamination site after a simulated terrorist attack. Simulations like these are preparing emergency responders for real disasters.

symptoms to look out for and how to report a possible out-break to the authorities.

Stockpiling medications and vaccines is a major compo-nent of plans for responding to an epidemic. Like in the smallpox scenario described in chapter 2, in 2001, the United States had only a few million doses of the smallpox vaccine. These doses were left over from the vaccination campaigns of the 1970s. The country now has enough doses to vaccinate all residents. These doses were manufactured in the last few years using modern production methods.

Scientists are currently working to develop vaccines for diseases that don't yet have any effective preventative treatment, and they are also working on improved vaccines for the diseases that do. But sometimes, a vaccine cannot be prepared before the outbreak of a disease. Influenza viruses constantly change their DNA. And when they change it enough, an existing vaccine is no longer effective. This is why people must get shots for the seasonal flu every year. Thus, if a bird flu outbreak occurs, a vaccine will not be immediately available. But researchers are developing quicker, better ways to make flu vaccines. These should help pharmaceutical companies create a bird flu vaccine faster than in the past.

Since a vaccine won't be immediately available, many countries have stockpiled antiviral drugs for use in a flu pandemic. Research into new and better antiviral drugs is also under way. Should a huge outbreak of a deadly disease occur, plans created by the United States detail how vaccines and medications will be distributed to the public.

Technology is also improving the monitoring of outbreaks. During the SARS outbreak in 2002–2003, the CDC and WHO set up a Web site for doctors to report on patients who might have SARS. Public health officials thus received information about new cases much faster than in the past. The Web site also allowed doctors to share information about how they were caring for patients. Within days or weeks, rather than

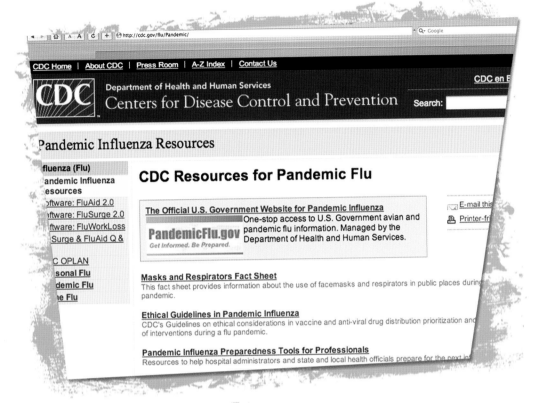

The Centers for Disease Control and Prevention Web site provides information about many diseases that could cause a pandemic. Particularly useful and updated information about swine and avian influenzas is available at http://www.pandemicflu.gov.

months, they learned which treatments were most effective. This almost certainly saved lives. Similar systems will be used in future widespread outbreaks of deadly diseases.

Of course, efforts by governments and other organizations are not enough. The next chapter looks at what individuals can do to prepare for a pandemic.

Chapter 4

WHAT YOU CAN DO TO FIGHT KILLER VIRUSES

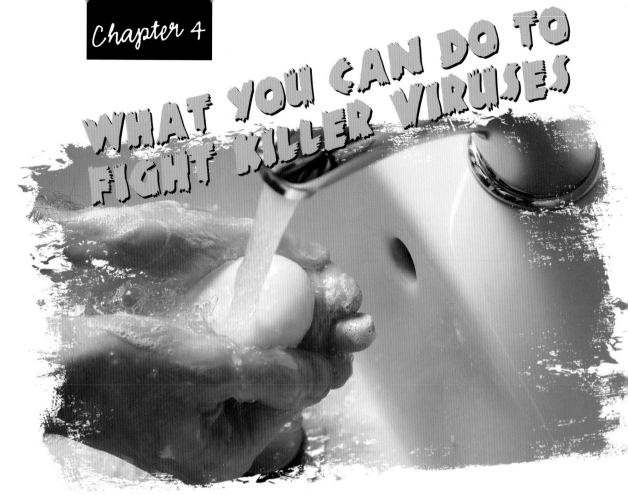

People can do some very simple things to help prevent disease. Handwashing only takes a minute but is quite effective.

Governments, the World Health Organization, and other groups have done a lot of work to prepare the world for a large outbreak of a deadly disease. But large-scale efforts are not the only option. In fact, they are far from enough. If a pandemic occurs, federal and state efforts will be essential. However, officials cannot be everywhere at once. It is important for individuals, families, and communities to make their own preparations for an epidemic.

Flushing Viruses Away

Although many diseases are spread by coughing and sneezing, not all are. Diseases that affect the digestive system are most commonly spread via the fecal-oral route. That is, people unknowingly ingest small amounts of feces (solid waste). This is one reason why it is so important for people to wash their hands after using the toilet. Also, people should put the lid down on a toilet before they flush it. Scientists have found that a flushing toilet can cause an aerosol of water and fecal matter to be propelled several feet into the air. Viruses in this aerosol may come into contact with eyes, nose, or the mouth, thus spreading illness.

Some pandemic preparation is similar to preparation for other kinds of emergencies, such as earthquakes, hurricanes, or terrorist attacks. Other preparations are simple hygiene practices that everyone learns as a child, but many don't practice as they get older. The rest of this chapter describes some of the basic, straightforward things that everyone can do, as well as ways to get involved in larger efforts to prevent or prepare for a pandemic.

Practice Good Personal Hygiene

Simple hygiene measures can help protect people from infectious diseases. Good hygiene makes it less likely that one person will pass on a disease to another. Hand washing is the single most important thing people can do. Public health officials suggest always washing one's hands after coughing, sneezing, or shaking hands with someone else. You can also use anti-bacterial wipes if you are not near a sink and soap.

Every cough and sneeze is a way for a virus to escape the body and find a new host. Public health officials no longer suggest that people use their hands to cover their mouth and nose while coughing or sneezing. Instead, cough or sneeze into the crook of your elbow if a tissue is not available. An arm is less likely to transmit viruses to various surfaces than a hand is. Used tissues should be thrown away immediately.

In general, people should avoid touching their eyes, mouth, and nose, particularly in public. Let's say that a student coughs or sneezes on a table in the cafeteria during lunch. The next kid who touches the table may get the virus on her hands. If she avoids touching her face until she washes her hands next, she is much less likely to introduce the virus into her body and become ill.

Finally, people who are sick should stay home from work and/or school. Many serious diseases start out just like a cold

Because the flu virus changes all the time, people must get flu shots every year. This is also why researchers can't create a vaccine for bird flu before an epidemic begins.

or the seasonal flu. Only after a few days or a week does it become apparent that the disease is much more serious. Of course, many diseases are contagious before symptoms arise, so staying home will not prevent all transmission. But it helps.

Stay Up to Date on Vaccinations

People should keep up to date on their recommended vaccinations, including booster shots in adulthood. The CDC provides vaccination schedules for children and adults on its Web site. It also suggests vaccinations for travelers.

Some diseases that occur rarely, if ever, in the United States are common in other areas of the world. Thus, before traveling to a foreign country, people may want or need additional vaccinations. People don't want to come down with yellow fever or another serious illness while on vacation. But people should also be wary of bringing a disease back to their hometown and starting an outbreak. Sometimes, these vaccines require weeks or months to take full effect. As a result, planning for trips should begin well in advance. Some health care providers specialize in travel medicine and stock vaccines for the diseases that travelers may encounter.

Use Caution Around Wild and Domestic Animals

Both wild and domestic animals act as reservoirs for many of the diseases that could cause serious outbreaks, including

In 2003, many people became ill with a virus called monkeypox, which is similar to smallpox. Researchers traced it from humans to prairie dogs that had been housed with Gambian giant rats.

bird flu. Thus, people should respect these animals and give them plenty of space.

When camping, hiking, and otherwise enjoying the outdoors, people should keep their distance from wild animals.

This is especially true for animals known to be disease reservoirs, such as mice, which are known to carry hantavirus. Contact with domestic animals should also be limited. People who live on, work at, or visit farms should take precautions, such as frequent hand washing and cleaning of shoes (to prevent tracking animal feces from place to place).

In addition, people should not buy exotic animals as pets or for food. Live wild birds are particularly of concern. In 2003, a monkeypox outbreak occurred in the Midwestern United States. The outbreak was eventually linked to pet prairie dogs that, before being shipped to pet stores, were housed with Gambian giant rats carrying the monkeypox virus. In addition, researchers eventually identified civet cats, which are eaten in China, as a likely animal reservoir for SARS. Reducing or eliminating the trade in exotic animals could help prevent outbreaks of killer viruses.

Support for efforts to preserve habitats for wild animals can also help prevent epidemics. As suburbs expand into formerly wild lands, and roads and developments chop habitats into smaller chunks, wild animals are more likely to come into contact with humans. Furthermore, reduction in the number of predators in an area by hunting or habitat destruction can allow the numbers of disease-bearing smaller animals to increase. Preserving habitats for animals isn't just good for them; it's good for people, too.

Prepare Poultry Carefully

Overcrowded poultry cages may be the breeding grounds for the next influenza epidemic. As described in chapter 2, the influenza virus affects the intestines of chickens, and fecal matter containing the virus can contaminate meat. Poultry and eggs can also transmit several other serious diseases. Thus, cooks need to be careful when preparing chicken, turkey, duck, and other birds.

Cooks should use separate cutting boards for meat and vegetables. Cutting boards, knives, utensils, hands, and other surfaces that come into contact with raw meat should be washed in hot, soapy water as soon as possible. Further disinfection with diluted bleach is recommended for cutting boards. Cooks should use a food thermometer to ensure that the meat reaches an internal temperature of at least 165 degrees Fahrenheit (74 degrees Celsius).

When possible, people should buy chicken, turkey, and other poultry from small family farms where the poultry is raised outside with lots of space ("free range"). This is important for two reasons. First, these uncrowded birds are less likely to be infected with and spread a serious flu virus. Second, as more consumers buy free-range chicken, more farms will raise birds this way. Alternatively, choosing not to eat poultry decreases your chances of encountering a bird flu virus.

Make a Pandemic Preparedness Plan

Many families have plans for emergencies such as a fire, earthquake, or hurricane. A pandemic preparedness plan is also essential. Many aspects of a pandemic preparedness plan will be the same as those for other emergencies. The Web site http://www.pandemicflu.gov, which incorporates information from many U.S. government agencies, is the place to start when preparing for a deadly disease outbreak.

Most stores use something called just-in-time inventory. This means that they generally have only a few days' worth of items in their stockrooms. If a pandemic interrupts the production and transport of basic consumer goods, local stores may run out of food, water, medicine, masks, and other supplies. Thus, it is important for every family to have their own supplies of these essential items. Two weeks' worth of food and bottled water is recommended. Families should keep several weeks' worth of prescription drugs, as well as some over-the-counter remedies. Soap, alcohol-based hand sanitizer, and facemasks are also crucial.

Buying all of these supplies at once may be financially difficult for some families. They may want to purchase just a few extra items on each shopping trip—three cans of tuna instead of two, for example. This gradually builds up emergency supplies. A backyard garden could also provide fresh vegetables and fruits during an emergency.

In addition to supplies, families need to plan if, how, and where they will isolate themselves in the event of an epidemic. Isolation is an important defense. Viruses have more trouble hopping from host to host when fewer people are around. Families who have cabins or second homes in remote areas may wish to move there if a pandemic occurs.

In early 2009, a new influenza virus linked to pigs affected people around the world. Known as swine flu, it infected tens of thousands of people, killed more than a hundred, and caused schools in several U.S. cities to close.

These cabins should be stocked with food, water, and medical supplies. Even if families remain in cities or suburbs, they will need to decide whether or not children will continue to go to school and adults to work.

Neighborhoods and towns should also have plans for what to do if a pandemic occurs. A pandemic will affect a lot of people in a lot of places, all at the same time. As a result, help from the federal or state government may be delayed or unavailable. All states have created pandemic preparedness plans, as have some major cities. These are available for viewing at http://www.pandemicflu.gov. The Web site also has suggestions for local pandemic preparation plans.

If an Outbreak Does Happen

If an epidemic occurs, whether as a result of a naturally occurring virus or a bioterrorist attack, the most important thing is to remain calm. Panic will only make things worse. People should follow the instructions of public health officials regarding vaccination, health care, and quarantine. But they should also be prepared to take care of themselves to avoid illness or death. The nightmare scenarios laid out in this book are unlikely to occur, but everyone should be prepared just in case a virus does get loose and unleashes deadly disease.

aerosol A particle mist that usually comes from a person coughing or sneezing.

bacteria Single-celled organisms, some of which cause disease.

bioterrorism The use of disease-causing bacteria and viruses as weapons.

Ebola A disease that causes victims to bleed profusely. Outbreaks have occurred mainly in Africa.

epidemic An outbreak of a disease that affects many people and can be spread from person to person.

hantavirus A disease carried by mice that can cause fluid buildup in the lungs.

hemorrhagic fever A disease that causes people to begin bleeding out of various orifices (body openings). Ebola and hantavirus are both hemorrhagic fevers.

immune system The system in the human body that fights disease.

influenza A respiratory illness that causes illness; also known as the flu.

outbreak A sudden emergence of a disease, often in a large number of people.

pandemic A global epidemic.

parasite An organism that cannot survive on its own and instead lives off of another organism.

pneumonia A bacterial infection of the lungs that may develop when the immune system is busy fighting a virus.

quarantine Isolation of people who are infected with a disease or have been exposed to a disease; this action is designed to stop the illness from spreading to others.

reproductive rate The average number of other people that
an ill person infects with a certain disease.

reservoir An animal that carries a virus that is not harmful to
the animal but can cause disease in humans.

severe acute respiratory syndrome (SARS) A disease that
causes cough, high fever, and fluid buildup in the lungs.
An epidemic of SARS occurred in 2003.

smallpox A disease that was wiped out in the 1970s but
could still be used in a bioterrorist attack.

supportive care Medical care that does not kill a disease but
helps a patient and his or her immune system remain
strong and healthy enough to fight against the illness.

vaccination The process of stimulating the immune system
with a weakened or dead virus so that it creates antibodies
that can one day fight against the actual virus.

virus An organism composed of nucleic acid and protein
that often causes disease.

American Public Health Association
800 I Street NW
Washington, DC 20001-3710
(202) 777-APHA
Web site: http://www.apha.org
The American Public Health Association helps protect communities from serious threats to health and promotes preventive health care.

American Society for Microbiology
1752 N Street NW
Washington, DC 20036
(202) 737-3600
Web site: http://www.asm.org
The American Society for Microbiology brings together researchers who work on viruses, bacteria, and other microorganisms, and helps communicate their findings to others.

Canadian Society of Microbiologists
CSM-SCM Secretariat
c/o Rofail Conference and Management Services
17 Dossetter Way
Ottawa, ON K1G 4S3
Canada
(613) 482-1337
Web site: http://www.csm-scm.org
The Canadian Society of Microbiologists is a collection of scientists who do research on microorganisms, including viruses and bacteria. The organization provides networking

opportunities and communicates this research to the general public.

Centers for Disease Control and Prevention (CDC)
1600 Clifton Road
Atlanta, GA 30333
(800) CDC-INFO (282-4636)
Web site: http://www.cdc.gov
The CDC is the primary U.S. government agency devoted to public health and epidemiology.

Federal Emergency Management Agency (FEMA)
500 C Street SW
Washington, DC 20472
(800) 646-2500
Web site: http://www.fema.gov
FEMA is the U.S. government agency that responds to major emergencies, such as a deadly pandemic.

Food and Agriculture Organization of the United Nations
Viale delle Terme di Caracalla
00153 Rome
Italy
Phone: 39 06 57051
Web site: http://www.fao.org
The Food and Agriculture Organization helps maintain a safe global food supply. It has been involved in work to prevent bird flu and other diseases that affect both food animals and humans.

Public Health Agency of Canada
130 Colonnade Road

A. L. 6501H
Ottawa, ON K1A 0K9
Canada
Web site: http://www.phac-aspc.gc.ca
The Public Health Agency of Canada responds to infectious
    disease outbreaks and provides information on a wide
    variety of illnesses.

World Health Organization (WHO)
Avenue Appia 20
1211 Geneva 27
Switzerland
Phone: 41 22 791 21 11
Web site: http://www.who.int
WHO responds to disease outbreaks around the world and is
    an important source of information during epidemics that
    cross national borders.

Web Sites

Due to the changing nature of Internet links, Rosen
Publishing has developed an online list of Web sites related
to the subject of this book. This site is updated regularly.
Please use this link to access this list:

http://www.rosenlinks.com/doom/viru

For Further Reading

Cobb, Vicki. *Your Body Battles a Cold*. Brookfield, CT: Millbrook Press, 2009.

Collier, James Lincoln. *The Empty Mirror*. New York, NY: Bloomsbury USA Children's Books, 2004.

Crumpton, Michael. *Bacteria and Viruses*. Logan, IA: Perfection Learning, 2007.

DeFelice, Cynthia. *The Apprenticeship of Lucas Whitaker*. New York, NY: Farrar, Straus, and Giroux, 2007.

Goldsmith, Connie. *Influenza: The Next Pandemic?* Minneapolis, MN: Twenty-First Century Books, 2006.

Grady, Denise. *Deadly Invaders: Virus Outbreaks Around the World, from Marburg Fever to Avian Flu*. Boston, MA: Kingfisher, 2006.

Moss, Jenny. *Winnie's War*. New York, NY: Walker Books for Young Readers, 2009.

Murphy, Jim. *An American Plague: The True and Terrifying Story of the Yellow Fever Epidemic of 1793*. New York, NY: Clarion Books, 2003.

Peters, Stephanie True. *The 1918 Influenza Pandemic*. Tarrytown, NY: Marshall Cavendish Children's Books, 2004.

Piddock, Charles. *Outbreaks: Science Seeks Safeguards for Global Health*. Des Moines, IA: National Geographic Children's Books, 2008.

Serradell, Joaquima. *SARS*. New York, NY: Chelsea House Publishers, 2005.

Walker, Richard. *Epidemics and Plagues*. Boston, MA: Kingfisher, 2007.

Centers for Disease Control and Prevention. "Emergency Preparedness and Response: Bioterrorism Agents/ Diseases." CDC.gov. Retrieved March 27, 2009 (http:// www.bt.cdc.gov/agent/agentlist-category.asp).

Centers for Disease Control and Prevention. "Emergency Preparedness and Response: Smallpox." CDC.gov. Retrieved March 27, 2009 (http://www.bt.cdc.gov/ agent/smallpox).

Centers for Disease Control and Prevention Special Pathogens Branch. "Known Cases and Outbreaks of Ebola Hemorrhagic Fever, in Chronological Order." CDC.gov, August 25, 2006. Retrieved March 24, 2008 (http://www.cdc.gov/ncidod/ dvrd/spb/mnpages/dispages/ebola/ebolatable.htm).

Greger, Michael. *Bird Flu: A Virus of Our Own Hatching*. New York, NY: Lantern Books, 2006.

Kolata, Gina. *Flu: The Story of the Great Influenza Pandemic of 1918 and the Search for the Virus That Caused It*. New York, NY: Farrar, Straus and Giroux, 1999.

Link, Kurt. *The Vaccine Controversy: The History, Use, and Safety of Vaccinations*. Westport, CT: Praeger Publishers, 2005.

McKenna, Maryn. *Beating Back the Devil: On the Front Lines with the Disease Detectives of the Epidemic Intelligence Service*. New York, NY: Free Press, 2004.

Oldstone, Michael B. A. *Viruses, Plagues, and History*. New York, NY: Oxford University Press, 1998.

Taubenberger, Jeffery K., and David M. Morens. "1918 Influenza: The Mother of All Pandemics." *Emerging Infectious Diseases*, January 2006. Retrieved March 11, 2009 (http://www.cdc.gov/ncidod/eid/vol12no01/05-0979.htm).

U.S. Department of Agriculture Food Safety and Inspection Service. "Fact Sheets: Safe Food Handling." USDA.gov, February 26, 2009. Retrieved March 15, 2009 (http://www.fsis.usda.gov/Fact_Sheets/Safe_Food_Handling_Fact_Sheets/index.asp).

U.S. Department of Health and Human Services. "Guidance on Antiviral Drug Use During an Influenza Pandemic." PandemicFlu.gov, January 2006. Retrieved March 20, 2009 (http://www.pandemicflu.gov/vaccine/antiviral_use.html).

U.S. Department of Health and Human Services. "Pandemic Flu Planning Checklist for Individuals and Families." PandemicFlu.gov, January 2006. Retrieved March 20, 2009 (http://www.pandemicflu.gov/plan/individual/checklist.html).

Walters, Mark Jerome. *Six Modern Plagues and How We Are Causing Them*. Washington, DC: Island Press, 2003.

World Health Organization. "Summary of Probable SARS Cases with Onset of Illness from 1 November 2002 to 31 July 2003." WHO.int, April 2004. Retrieved March 2009 (http://www.who.int/csr/sars/country/table2004_04_21/en/index.html).

Zelicoff, Alan P., and Michael Bellomo. *Microbe: Are We Ready for the Next Plague?* New York, NY: American Management Association, 2005.

About the Author

Linley Erin Hall is a science writer and editor in Berkeley, California. She has a bachelor's degree in chemistry from Harvey Mudd College and a certificate in science communication from the University of California–Santa Cruz. Hall has written on several topics related to infectious diseases, including seasonal flu shots, hepatitis treatment, and the bacterium that causes stomach ulcers. This is her seventh book for Rosen Publishing, and she came down with the flu while writing it. She is also the author of *Who's Afraid of Marie Curie? The Challenges Facing Women in Science and Technology*.

Photo Credits

Cover, p. 1 Luis Acosta/AFP/Getty Images; pp. 4–5 National Museum of Health and Medicine; pp. 6, 16 Joe Raedle/Getty Images; p. 8 © www.istockphoto.com/Guillermo Perales Gonzalez; p. 10 Cheryl Tryon/CDC; p. 12 Dr. Scott Smith/CDC; p. 14 © SPL/Photo Researchers, Inc.; p. 17 Judy Schmidt/CDC; pp. 18–19 © Custom Medical Stock Photo; p. 21 Roslan Rahman/AFP/Getty Images; pp. 24–25, 48–49, 52–53 © AP Images; p. 26 Sybil McCarro/U.S. Navy/Getty Images; pp. 28–29 Mike Clarke/AFP/Getty Images; p. 32 © www.istockphoto.com/Christopher Badzioch; p. 36 Carlos Palma/AFP/Getty Images; p. 39 William Thomas Cain/Getty Images; pp. 40–41 Scott Olson/Getty Images; p. 44 © www.istockphoto.com/domin_domin; pp. 46–47 Robert Giroux/Getty Images.

Designer: Sam Zavieh; Photo Researcher: Amy Feinberg